American Symbols

The Lincoln Memorial

by Terri DeGezelle

Consultant:
Melodie Andrews, Ph.D.
Associate Professor of Early American History
Minnesota State University, Mankato

Capstone

First Facts is published by Capstone Press
151 Good Counsel Drive, P.O. Box 669, Mankato, Minnesota 56002
www.capstonepress.com

Library of Congress Cataloging-in-Publication Data
DeGezelle, Terri 1955–
    The Lincoln memorial / by Terri DeGezelle.
    p. cm.—(First Facts. American symbols)
    Summary: A simple introduction to the Lincoln Memorial, including its history,
designer, construction, location, and importance as a symbol of the United States.
    Includes bibliographical references and index.
    ISBN 0-7368-2529-0 (hardcover)
    1. Lincoln Memorial (Washington, D.C.)—Juvenile literature. 2. Lincoln, Abraham,
1809–1865—Monuments—Washington (D.C.)—Juvenile literature. 3. Washington (D.C.)—
Buildings, structures, etc.—Juvenile literature. [1. Lincoln Memorial (Washington, D.C.)
2. National monuments.] I. Title. II. Series. American symbols (Mankato, Minn.)
F203.4.L73D44 2004
973.7'092—dc21
                                        2003011501

Editorial Credits
Roberta Schmidt, editor; Linda Clavel, series designer; Molly Nei, book designer and
    illustrator; Kelly Garvin and Scott Thoms, photo researchers; Eric Kudalis and
    Karen Risch, product planning editors

Photo Credits
Bruce Coleman Inc./Norman Owen Tomalin, 15, 16–17
Corel, 6–7
Digital Stock, 5, 19
Folio Inc./Alan Goldstein, 13
Getty Images/Hulton Archive, 9, 18, 20
Library of Congress, 11
PhotoDisc Inc., cover (left); Hisham F. Ibrahim, cover (right)

1 2 3 4 5 6 09 08 07 06 05 04

Table of Contents

Lincoln Memorial Fast Facts

- The Lincoln Memorial honors Abraham Lincoln. He was the 16th president of the United States.

- Work began on the Lincoln Memorial on February 12, 1914. This day was the 105th anniversary of Abraham Lincoln's birthday.

- The statue of Lincoln is made of 28 blocks of white marble.

- The Lincoln Memorial has 36 white columns. These columns stand for the 36 states that were in the nation when Lincoln died.

- The Lincoln Memorial has 56 stone steps. These steps stand for Lincoln's age of 56 years when he died.

- The Lincoln Memorial was dedicated on May 30, 1922.

Symbol of Freedom and Unity

The Lincoln **Memorial** is a **symbol** of **freedom** and **unity**. The memorial reminds people of President Abraham Lincoln. Lincoln believed that all people should be free. He also worked hard to keep the United States together.

Fun Fact:
American architect Henry Bacon designed the Lincoln Memorial.

Lincoln and the Civil War

Abraham Lincoln was the president of the United States during the Civil War (1861–1865). Lincoln was a great leader. He helped to end slavery in the United States. Lincoln also worked to end the Civil War. He tried to bring the North and the South back together.

 Fun Fact:
Lincoln started school when he was eight years old.
He had to walk 1.5 miles (2.4 kilometers) to the school.

9

A Memorial Building

After Lincoln died, Congress decided to build a **monument** to remember him. In 1902, a place for the memorial was chosen in Washington, D.C.

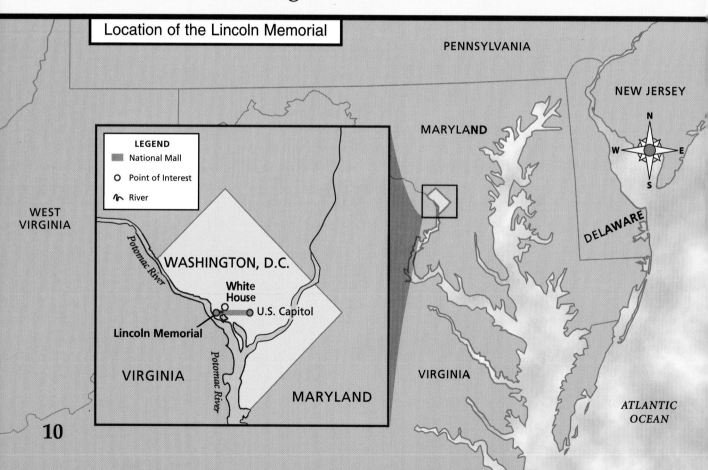

Location of the Lincoln Memorial

LEGEND
- National Mall
- O Point of Interest
- ⌁ River

PENNSYLVANIA

NEW JERSEY

MARYLAND

WEST VIRGINIA

WASHINGTON, D.C.

Potomac River

White House

○ U.S. Capitol

Lincoln Memorial

VIRGINIA

Potomac River

MARYLAND

DELAWARE

VIRGINIA

ATLANTIC OCEAN

N
W E
S

Work on the Lincoln Memorial began in 1914. Workers used stone from different parts of the United States to build the memorial. It was finished in eight years.

The Statue of Abraham Lincoln

An important part of the memorial is the **statue** of Lincoln. Daniel Chester French **designed** the statue. He wanted to show that Lincoln was a strong, kind person. The statue's left hand is in a fist. It stands for strength. The right hand is open. It stands for kindness.

 Fun Fact:
The statue of Lincoln is 19 feet (5.8 meters) tall.
It weighs 175 tons (159 metric tons).

13

The Walls of the Memorial

Important items are on the walls of the memorial. Two of Lincoln's speeches are carved into the walls. Each speech has a painting above it. One painting shows slaves being freed. The other painting shows people from the North and the South joining hands.

 Fun Fact:
The Gettysburg Address is one of Lincoln's most famous speeches. It has been translated into 29 languages.

FOUR SCORE AND SEVEN YEARS
AGO OUR FATHERS BROUGHT FORTH
ON THIS CONTINENT A NEW NATION
CONCEIVED IN LIBERTY AND DEDICA-
TED TO THE PROPOSITION THAT ALL
MEN ARE CREATED EQUAL.
NOW WE ARE ENGAGED IN A GREAT
CIVIL WAR TESTING WHETHER THAT
NATION OR ANY NATION SO CON-
CEIVED AND SO DEDICATED CAN LONG
ENDURE . WE ARE MET ON A GREAT
BATTLEFIELD OF THAT WAR . WE HAVE
COME TO DEDICATE A PORTION OF
THAT FIELD AS A FINAL RESTING
PLACE FOR THOSE WHO HERE GAVE
THEIR LIVES THAT THAT NATION
MIGHT LIVE . IT IS ALTOGETHER FIT-
TING AND PROPER THAT WE SHOULD
DO THIS . BUT IN A LARGER SENSE
WE CAN NOT DEDICATE ~ WE CAN NOT
CONSECRATE ~ WE CAN NOT HALLOW ~
THIS GROUND . THE BRAVE MEN LIV ~
ING AND DEAD WHO STRUGGLED HERE
HAVE CONSECRATED IT FAR ABOVE
OUR POOR POWER TO ADD OR DETRACT .
THE WORLD WILL LITTLE NOTE NOR
LONG REMEMBER WHAT WE SAY HERE
BUT IT CAN NEVER FORGET WHAT THEY
DID HERE . IT IS FOR US THE LIVING
RATHER TO BE DEDICATED HERE TO
THE UNFINISHED WORK WHICH THEY
WHO FOUGHT HERE HAVE THUS FAR
SO NOBLY ADVANCED . IT IS RATHER FOR
US TO BE HERE DEDICATED TO THE
GREAT TASK REMAINING BEFORE US ~
THAT FROM THESE HONORED DEAD
WE TAKE INCREASED DEVOTION TO
THAT CAUSE FOR WHICH THEY GAVE THE
LAST FULL MEASURE OF DEVOTION ~
THAT WE HERE HIGHLY RESOLVE THAT
THESE DEAD SHALL NOT HAVE DIED IN
VAIN ~ THAT THIS NATION UNDER GOD
SHALL HAVE A NEW BIRTH OF FREEDOM ~
AND THAT GOVERNMENT OF THE PEOPLE
BY THE PEOPLE FOR THE PEOPLE SHALL
NOT PERISH FROM THE EARTH .

The Lincoln Memorial Today

The Lincoln Memorial is an important American symbol. It is shown on the back of the U.S. penny and the $5 bill. Millions of people visit the Lincoln Memorial each year. They think of Abraham Lincoln and his fight for freedom and unity.

 Fun Fact:
The Lincoln Memorial was put on the back of the penny in 1959.

Time Line

1809—Abraham Lincoln is born in Kentucky.

1865—Lincoln dies.

1860—Lincoln is elected president of the United States.

1861–1865—The North and the South fight the Civil War.

1914—Work begins on the Lincoln Memorial.

1902—A place for the memorial is chosen in Washington, D.C.

1922—The Lincoln Memorial is dedicated.

19

On August 28, 1963, Dr. Martin Luther King Jr. gave a speech on the steps of the Lincoln Memorial. At least 250,000 people were there. King's speech was called "I Have a Dream." He spoke about equal rights for African Americans and all people.

Hands On: Look at the Memorial

The Lincoln Memorial is pictured on the back of the penny and the $5 bill. Use a magnifying glass to look at the images on these items.

What You Need

penny (newer is better)
$5 bill
hand-held magnifying glass

What You Do

1. Put the penny and the $5 bill face-up on a flat surface, such as a desk or a table.
2. Hold the magnifying glass over the penny. Whose face is on the front of the penny?
3. Look at the $5 bill. Who is pictured on the front? How does this image of Lincoln look different from the one on the penny?
4. Turn the $5 bill over. Look at the Lincoln Memorial pictured there. Do you see anything between the pillars of the memorial? Look at it through the magnifying glass.
5. Turn the penny over. Can you see the statue? Put the magnifying glass over the penny. Can you see the statue now?

Glossary

design (di-ZINE)—to make a plan for how to build something

freedom (FREE-duhm)—the right to live the way you want

memorial (muh-MOR-ee-uhl)—something that is built or done to help people remember a person or event

monument (MON-yuh-muhnt)—a statue or building that is meant to remind people of an event or a person

statue (STACH-oo)—something carved or shaped out of stone, wood, or other material

symbol (SIM-buhl)—an object that stands for something else

unity (YOO-ni-tee)—being together as one

Read More

Deady, Kathleen W. *The Lincoln Memorial.* National Landmarks. Mankato, Minn.: Bridgestone Books, 2002.

Gilmore, Frederic. *The Lincoln Memorial: A Great President Remembered.* Chanhassen, Minn.: Child's World, 2001.

Internet Sites

FactHound offers a safe, fun way to find Internet sites related to this book. All of the sites on FactHound have been researched by our staff.

Here's how:
1. Visit *www.facthound.com*
2. Type in this special code **0736825290** for age-appropriate sites. Or enter a search word related to this book for a more general search.
3. Click on the **Fetch It** button.

FactHound will fetch the best sites for you!

Index